Carving Undercover
SANTAS

Carving Undercover
SANTAS

13 Projects in Wood
with Patterns and Painting Instructions

Russell Scott

Fox Chapel
PUBLISHING

© 2019 by Russell Scott and Fox Chapel Publishing Company, Inc., 903 Square Street, Mount Joy, PA 17552.

Carving Undercover Santas is an original work, first published in 2019 by Fox Chapel Publishing Company, Inc. The patterns contained herein are copyrighted by the author. Readers may make copies of these patterns for personal use. The patterns themselves, however, are not to be duplicated for resale or distribution under any circumstances. Any such copying is a violation of copyright law.

ISBN 978-1-4971-0006-0

The Cataloging-in-Publication Data is on file with the Library of Congress.

All text and step-by-step carving photography by Russell Scott
Studio photography by Mike Mahalo
Patterns by Carolyn Mosher
Shutterstock: ff-photo/cover background, nito/black apron, Volodymyr Krasyuk/first aid kit, James McDowall/vinyl gloves, JAROON MAGNUCH/cloth gloves, telensfix/safety glasses

To learn more about the other great books from Fox Chapel Publishing, or to find a retailer near you, call toll-free 800-457-9112 or visit us at *www.FoxChapelPublishing.com*.

We are always looking for talented authors. To submit an idea, please send a brief inquiry to acquisitions@foxchapelpublishing.com.

Printed in China
First printing

12

36

52

62

70

Contents

Introduction

"You'd better watch out, you'd better not cry," is a warning from the old song "Santa Claus Is Comin' to Town," written by John Frederick Coots and Haven Gillespie and first sung on the radio in November 1934. Or better yet, Santa would say, "Remember, I'm always watching." Santa Claus is a legendary figure tasked with bringing gifts to well-behaved (good or nice) children on Christmas Eve. I have always taken that warning seriously as I didn't want to be left out of the gift receiving.

But how does Santa know if children have been good? By going undercover, of course! Disguised as a businessman, park ranger, police officer, lifeguard, nurse, fireman, lifeguard, or someone else, Santa is able to watch for good or nice children. Santas, or his elves, are all around us keeping a watchful eye on us all.

In his later years, my father grew a white beard and had a rotund belly and a twinkle in his eye. Once, while waiting in line at the checkout counter at the grocery store, Dad observed a child in the cart in front of him making a ruckus and drawing a lot of attention to his obviously frustrated, overwrought and embarrassed mother. My father gave the child a look, raised his eyebrows and stated, "Remember, I'm always watching." The child's eyes grew round. My father didn't say another word but gave a stern look. The child immediately quieted down. The grateful mother looked at dad and whispered, "Thank you."

Dad continued his fun at playing Santa as a member of the Moose Lodge in St. Paul, Minnesota. He dressed as Santa each year, in a beautiful costume, to greet children and grandchildren of lodge members during a special event with Santa. He even had a special Santa chair that he reupholstered in red velvet for the annual event.

When Santa Came to the Meeting

My oldest brother, Rodney, posed as Santa for me as a child. When I was a very young cub scout we gathered in the elementary school gym for the annual meeting. We were told Santa was coming and would bring little white bags with candy for the kids. The meeting

"How does Santa know if children have been good?
By going undercover, of course!"

The meeting grew long, I grew bored, and my attention drifted until I remembered that Santa was coming with treats. I quickly straightened up, not wanting to miss out on the special treat of seeing Santa. At the end of the meeting the leader said we had to sing a song in order to get Santa to come in and we had to sing loudly. The first song was "Rudolf the Red-nosed Reindeer." When we finished, the leader looked to the door but Santa was not there. The leader told us we had not sung loud enough. So next we sang "Jingle Bells" really loudly. But still no Santa. I grew worried. Was the big guy really coming or had something gone wrong? The next song we sang at the top of our lungs was "Santa

Claus is Coming to Town." This was obviously the key, and sure enough, Santa appeared. He walked to the front of the group and we all lined up to wait our turn to greet him. When I got to the front of the line I noticed Santa's voice was not a deep adult voice but sounded more like a teenager's. When it was my turn to speak to Santa he called me by my nickname, Rusty. I was elated. How did he know my name? It had to be the real Santa. I was so happy until my next oldest brother, Rick, came over and told me that Santa was really Rodney. At first I didn't believe Rick. But on closer examination of Santa I came to realize it was true. I felt betrayed. But I quickly recovered when I was awarded the white bag of candy. This was my first taste of Santa going undercover. After all, the big guy couldn't possibly be everywhere, all the time, could he? Nowadays Rodney no longer needs to wear a fake beard or padding to complete his disguise as Santa to his grandchildren.

Not Just Males

Undercover Santa is not restricted to males. My mother-in-law was another undercover Santa. Genevieve was a farmer, a quilter, and a devoted mother and grandmother. Every year, well into her 90s, she would make a long list of all of her children, their spouses, grandchildren, great grandchildren, and great, great grandchildren, to make sure she had a gift for each one, numbering over a hundred people. She loved Christmas and didn't want to miss a single person. Each year in the fall she would gather apples from her trees and make dozens of apple pies to freeze and give as gifts to her family members. She also

WOODCARVING SAFETY

I always make a point to instruct the students in my carving class to look closely at the carving knife. They need to know which side of the blade is sharp since a carving knife is not the same as a sharp kitchen knife. In one of the first carving classes I took there was a young man who did not pay attention to which side was sharp and immediately cut his thumb.

I also tell my students to practice using their wrist in a rotation to make cuts into the wood and not take huge sweeping motions to cut. The smaller wrist motion gives them more control of the knife and is safer.

made strawberry and raspberry jams. She was definitely an undercover Santa.

As a Santa carver I often find myself looking at the people I meet in stores, restaurants, and events to see if I can spot an undercover Santa. After all, they are all around us and are always watching.

SAFETY TIPS FOR HAND CARVING

Eyewear—Safety glasses with side shields provide protection for the eyes but leave skin unprotected. Prescription glasses are not sufficient. Use safety goggles while handling liquids.

First Aid Kit—To be used for minor injuries. Include bandages, gauze, and tweezers.

Safety Glove—Kevlar threaded gloves are necessary when holding small woodcarvings to help prevent cuts to the hands or fingers. Leather gloves are useful when using the knife or chisel or while handling power tools.

Vinyl Gloves—For handling paint, oils, turpentine or mineral spirits. Latex gloves sometimes produce skin reactions.

Work Aprons—Heavy duty cloth is acceptable for carving operations and to protect the arms and legs during power tool and chain saw use.

PROJECTS

Chef Santa

Not only do I make sure children eat their vegetables, I also encourage them to eat healthy fats and proteins, and to cut down on sugar and carbs. Parents have a big role to play in their children's diets, of course, and I always say to follow common sense—and the USDA's dietary guidelines.

The step-by-step instructions for the Chef Santa demonstrate how to carve eye sockets, nostrils, hair, and beards. It serves as the general template for carving Santa's facial features.

Add Color

PAINTING

Titanium white (Americana)

Primary blue (Americana)

Ebony black (Americana)

Santa flesh (Ceramcoat)

French blue (FolkArt)

Dolphin gray (Americana)

Burnt sienna (Americana) and Santa flesh mixture

FINISHING
- Deft Clear Wood Finish Satin
- Watco Wax—mixture of neutral and dark

Front

Back

Left side

Right side

START SHAPING THE FACE

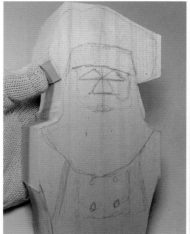

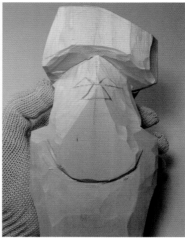

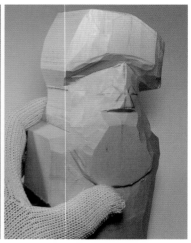

1. Pencil in the face as shown to get an understanding how the face would fit.

2. Cut out the chef's hat and bring the centerline to a sharp edge. Draw back in the eye socket and nose lines.

3. Use your knife and create a large stop cut and cut up to the bottom of the nose.

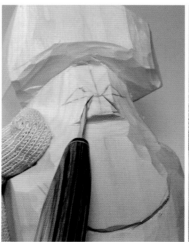

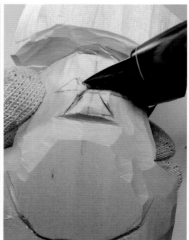

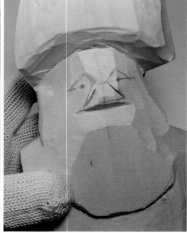

4. Draw dots for the eyeballs on the eye line. Firmly, cut down on the eye/nose lines toward the eyeball, away from the nose and eyebrows.

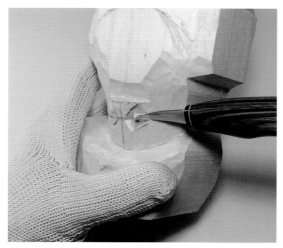

5. Make chip cuts as shown on the side of the nose to the eye socket.

6. Carve out the eye sockets down to the eye line.

7. Carve out the eye sockets on the other line, repeating the last two steps.

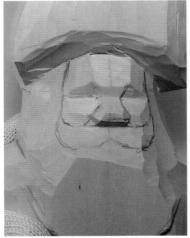

8. Draw in the face and mustache.

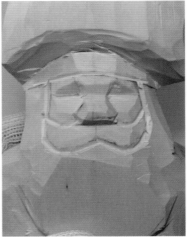

9. Use a V tool to gouge in the mustache.

10. Use a knife to make stop cuts along the bottom of the mustache and side of the face, and cut out the side of the face as shown.

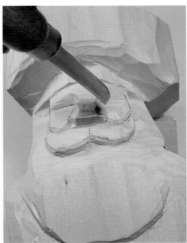

11. Press down on the side of the nose with a medium size #9 chisel to form the nostrils.

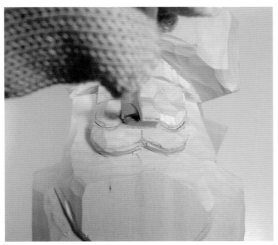

12. Remove the cut wood from the nostrils.

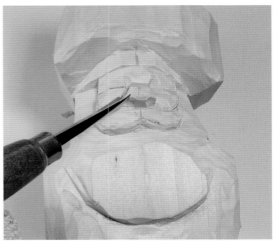

13. Use the medium size #9 chisel to cut along the side of the nose from the tip to the eye socket.

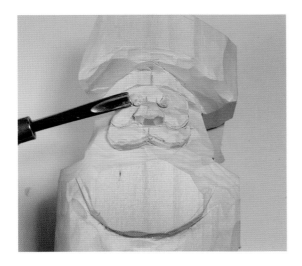

14. Use the medium size #9 chisel to cut along the top of the eye socket (under the eyebrow from the side, up in the middle of the stroke, and down into the wood at the bridge of the nose, forming a bulge in the center).

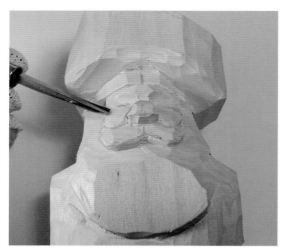

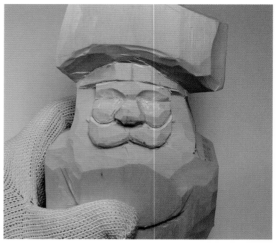

15. Use the same #9 chisel to shape the base of the nose and round the upper lid of the eye socket to the nose, forming a bulge in the center.

16. Here is the face as shown after the use of the medium size #9 chisel.

CARVE THE EARS

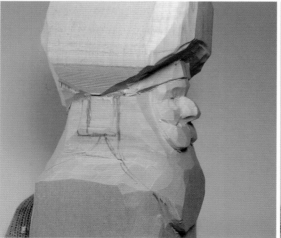

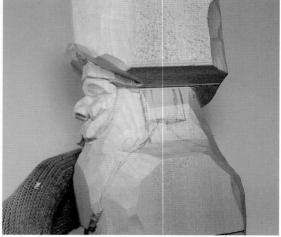

17. Draw in squares on both sides of the face to position the ear on both sides. The front line of the ear generally starts in the center of the face to back of the skull but bring that line a bit forward to compensate for the extra hair depth.

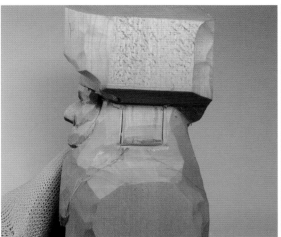

18. Use a V tool and cut out the pencil marks for the ear.

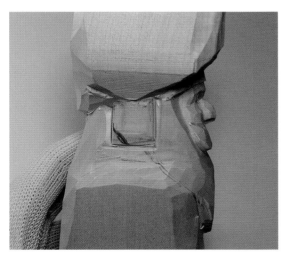

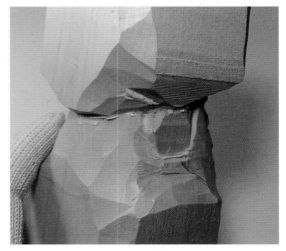

19. Draw the shape of the ear.

20. Undercut the back of the ear.

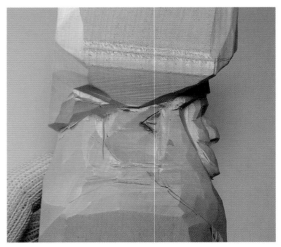

21. Carve the front base of the ear down to the sideburns.

22. Draw a V on the ear base level with the eye line. Create a deep undercut along the V.

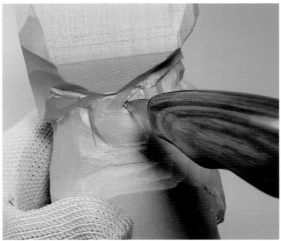

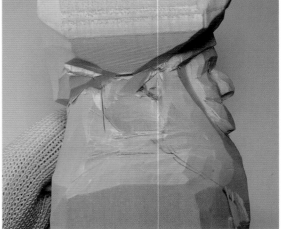

23. Create a deep undercut and remove the tip of the V as shown. This is the "listening" hole.

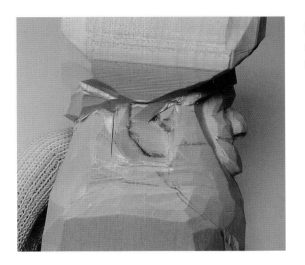

24. Pencil in and cut out the desired shape of the ear.

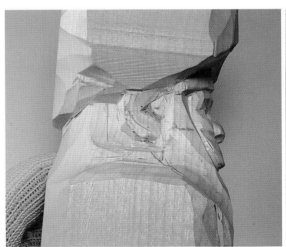 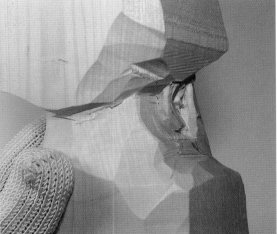

25. Pencil in and V cut a C line near the edge of the ear.

26. Use your knife to shape the nose.

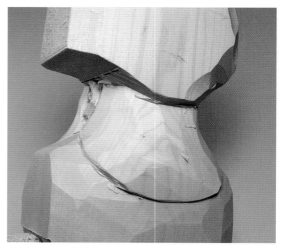

27. Shape the back of the hair to the desired length.

28. Draw a small semicircle under the mustache for the mouth. Use a knife to gouge out the hole in the mouth.

29. Undercut the beard to the bottom of the mouth, bringing the bottom lip up.

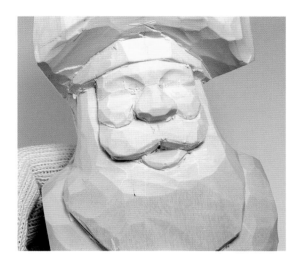

30. Use the tip of the knife to carve out the hole for the mouth (careful not to be careless and break the tip of the knife).

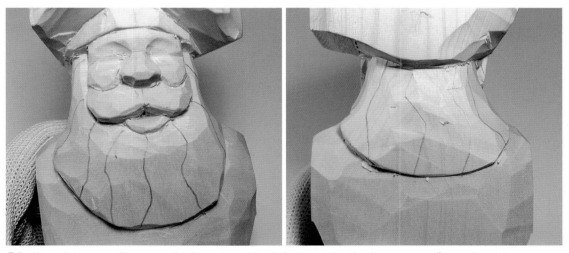

31. Pencil in wavy lines on the beard and back hair. Make the lines come from the side of the face.

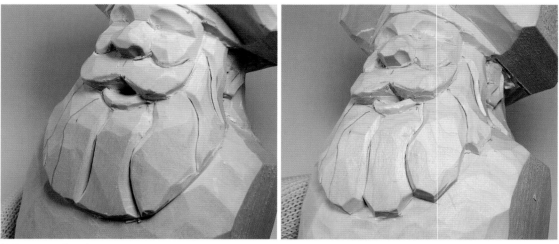

32. Use a knife to make straight cuts drawn by the pencil. Use a knife and cut beard segments to points.

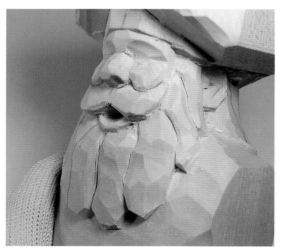

33. Use a knife to cut dents on both sides of the beard segments.

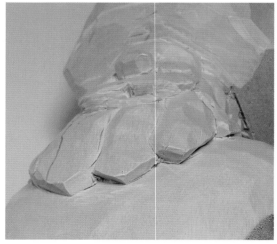

34. Use a knife to undercut the tips of the beard segments to bring them out.

35. Use a V tool and cut out definitions of the beard. Do not carve straight lines. Occasionally V cut crisscross lines to break up any parallel lines and make the beard scruffier.

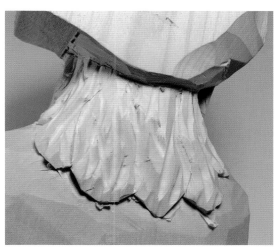

36. Back of the head.

37. Use a V tool and cut out definitions of the mustache.

38. With a pencil, draw in the buttons, edge of the shirt, and the edge of the apron.

39. Use a V tool and cut out the pencil marks of the buttons, edge of the shirt, and the edge of the apron.

40. Use a knife to cut back the shirt and bring the buttons and apron forward.

41. Round out the top of the hat.

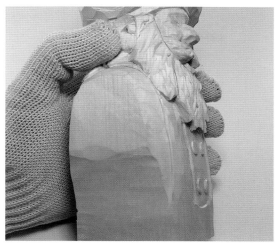

42. Use a knife to cut out the saw marks on the side of the bust.

43. Cut back the floppy top of the hat to give more on the headband.

44. Pencil in fold separations on the floppy top.

45. Use a knife to cut out deep cuts, then use chisels to shape the floppy separations.

 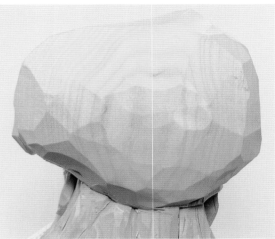

46. Cut top down so the floppy part falls (or make a desired shape).

47. Redraw the eye line. Make equal marks the same width as the base of the nose for each eye width.

48. Use a pencil to draw in the eye as shown. Use a knife and firmly cut down on the eye line.

49. Make chip cuts on both sides of the eyeball.

50. Round the upper eyeball.

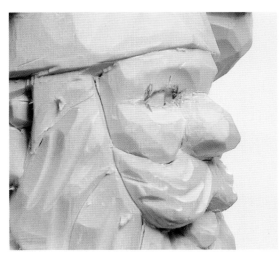

51. Round out the lower eyeball.

52. Bring up the eyebrow as shown.

53. With a pencil, draw in the eyelids then use a V tool to chisel them out.

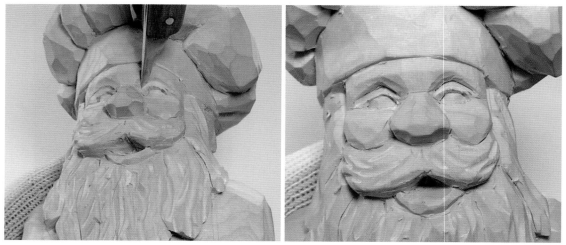

54. Use the tip of your knife to dig a sharp V cut to bring out the eyelids.

55. With a pencil, draw in the eyebrow crease.

56. Use the same #9 chisel to press down on the forehead for the eyebrows.

57. Use the same #9 chisel and a knife and clean out the eyebrow crease.

58. Use a knife to cut back the forehead to shape the eyebrow bone as shown.

59. Use a V tool to put in his eyebrow hair.

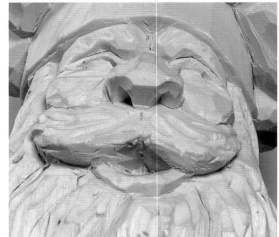

60. Use a knife to cut out the nostril holes. First cut the outside, then make the second cut from the inside so you won't cut off the side of the nose.

61. Finished.

CHEF SANTA PATTERN

Front

Left Side

Right Side

Back

Park Ranger Santa

I work for the National Park Service and my job is to keep trees, animals, rocks, waterways, and people safe. My crisp uniform and hat inspires children to be on their best behavior. In addition, I know all about the national park where I work, and can answer questions about history, animals, ecology, forests, and just about everything else—try me!

The step-by-step instructions for the Park Ranger Santa demonstrate how to paint the complete Santa figure. It serves as the general template for painting all of the undercover Santas. For my advanced tips on painting, see page 92.

Add Color

PAINTING

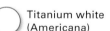

- Tomato red (Anita's)
- Suede (Craft Smart)
- Earth brown (Anita's)
- Light avocado green (Americana)
- Ivory (Ceramcoat)
- French blue (FolkArt)
- Titanium white (Americana)
- Santa flesh (Ceramcoat)
- Bayberry (FolkArt)
- Burnt sienna (Americana)
- True blue (Americana)
- Ebony black (Americana)

FINISHING

- Deft Clear Wood Finish Satin
- Watco Wax, a mixture of neutral and dark

Front

Back

Left side

Right side

PAINTING YOUR WOODCARVING

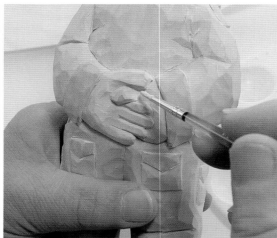

1. Mix two drops of Santa flesh paint to 1 tablespoon of water. Paint the face, ears, hands, and any other flesh parts.

2. Use a small brush and white paint straight out of the bottle to paint the eyes.

3. While we wait for the paint on the eyes to dry, mix three drops of dolphin gray paint to 1 teaspoon of water. Paint the beard with the watery mix.

4. Paint the eyebrow with the dolphin gray paint.

5. While we wait for the paint on the beard and eyebrows to dry, paint the iris with the desired iris color using a small liner brush. I used French blue.

6. Paint in the pupil with black paint straight out of the bottle using a liner brush.

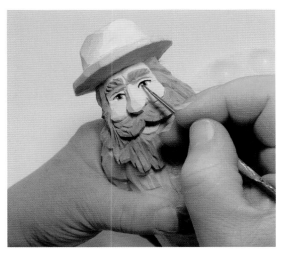

7. Paint a dot for the light reflection on the upper left side of the iris with white paint straight out of the bottle.

8. Back to the beard and eyebrows. Brush on ivory paint straight out of the bottle using a dry brush technique to show the dolphin gray between the cut marks.

9. When that dries, brush on white using a dry brush technique on top of the beard. This paint is also out of the bottle.

10. The face and beard so far.

11. Paint the mouth with burnt sienna and flesh color mixed.

12. Paint the hat with mix of one-part ivory paint to two parts water.

13. Paint the shirt with a mix of one part suede paint to two parts water. Paint the pants with a mix of one part light avocado green to two parts water, and the shoes and belt with a mix of one part earth brown to two parts water. Let the base paints dry.

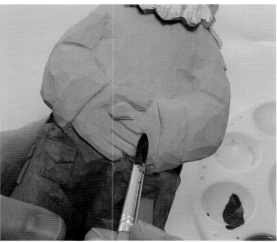

14. For the shading, mix three drops of burnt sienna paint with a tablespoon of water. Paint the face, ears, hands, and any other flesh parts. This wash adds an extra depth to the base paint.

15. Paint the cheeks and nose with burnt sienna with less water mixed in.

16. Quickly use your water and burnt sienna wash mix to pull the thick paint away as shown.

17. Paint burnt sienna out of the bottle along the eyelid and use your water and burnt sienna wash mix to pull the thick paint out, leaving the deep crevice with the dark burnt sienna.

18. Paint burnt sienna out of the bottle inside and outside of the ear and use your water and burnt sienna wash mix to pull the thick paint out leaving the deep crevice with the dark burnt sienna.

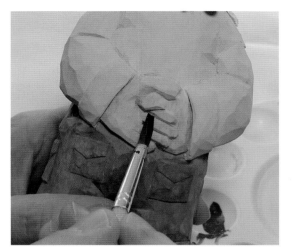

19. Paint burnt sienna out of the bottle between the fingers, near the sleeve cuff, and under the hands near the pants. Use your water and burnt sienna wash mix to pull the thick paint out, leaving the deep crevice with the dark burnt sienna.

20. Use your burnt sienna wash to paint the hat and shirt.

21. Paint on the creases with burnt sienna straight out of the bottle.

22. Quickly use your water and burnt sienna wash mix to pull the thick paint up as shown. Do small portions of the figure at a time so the paint straight out of the bottle will not dry where you don't want shade.

23. The shirt is complete.

24. Now you will shade the hat with your burnt sienna wash. Use your burnt sienna straight out of the bottle and paint under the hat. Quickly use your water and burnt sienna wash mix to pull the thick paint up as shown.

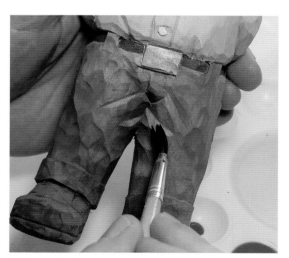

25. Wash the pants with true blue, two drops to one tablespoon mix.

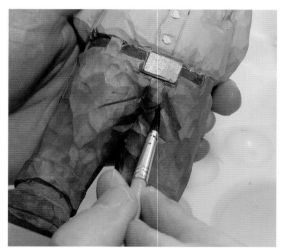

26. Paint on the creases with true blue straight out of the bottle.

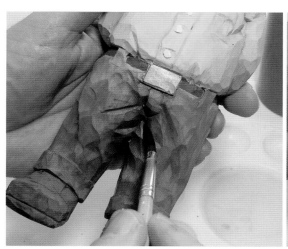 

27. Quickly use your water and true blue wash mix to pull the thick paint up as shown. Complete small portions of the figure at a time so the paint straight out of the bottle will not dry where you don't want shade.

28. Wash the shoes with black two drops to one tablespoon mix.

29. Paint on the creases with black straight out of the bottle.

30. Quickly use your water and black wash mix to pull the thick paint up as shown. Complete small portions of the figure at a time so the paint straight out of the bottle will not dry where you don't want shade.

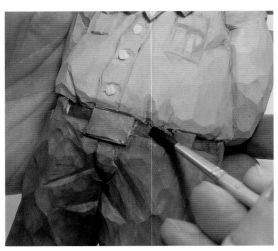

31. Wash the belt with black two drops to one tablespoon mix.

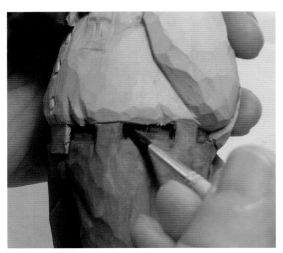

32. Paint on the creases with black straight out of the bottle.

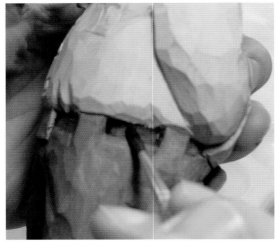

33. Quickly use your water and black wash mix to pull the thick paint up as shown. Complete small portions of the figure at a time so the paint straight out of the bottle will not dry where you don't want shade.

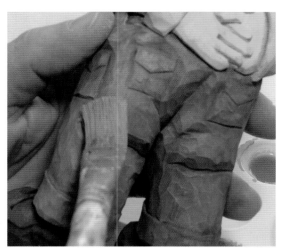

34. Use a clean, dry horsehair brush to highlight the shirt using the dry brush technique. Use Santa flesh straight out of the bottle. Wipe the brush on a rag or paper towel to remove most of the paint. Very lightly brush on the paint, only applying paint to the higher cut marks to highlight them.

35. Use a clean, dry horsehair brush to highlight the pants. Use bayberry straight out of the bottle. Wipe the brush on a rag or paper towel in an attempt to remove most of the paint. Very lightly brush on the paint, only applying paint to the higher cut marks to highlight them.

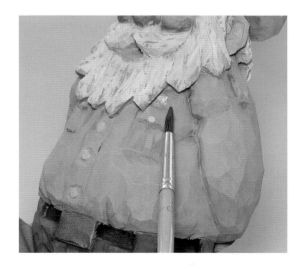

36. Use a small brush and paint on his badge with gold paint out of the bottle. Also paint the buttons on the shirt and pants pockets and the buttons on the collar straps. Your carving is now painted. Allow the paint to dry and spray with satin or matte finish for protection.

ANTIQUING YOUR WOODCARVING

37. Liberally apply a Watco wax mix of three-fourths neutral and one-fourth dark.

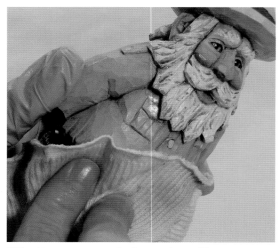

38. Use a cotton cloth to wipe off the excess wax.

39. Wipe the excess wax off the brush. Use a brush to pull out all the excess wax into the crevices and make sure the entire carving has an even amount of wax on the surface. Let the carving dry for a day. Use a clean stiff-bristled shoe brush to give the carving an even glow while removing any waxy residue from the crevices.

PARK RANGER SANTA PATTERN

Front

Left Side

Right Side

Back

Toy Store Manager Santa

Owning and managing a toy store has to be the best job in the world. Most of my time is spent in the office running my business, but I also take time out to go out onto the sales floor where I can play with the toys and interact with children, listening to their thoughts about which toys are the most fun. Sure, the kids can get rowdy and loud, but isn't that part of the fun?

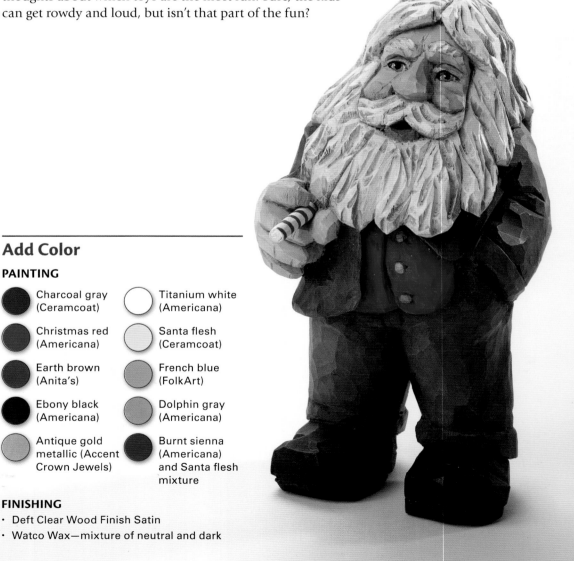

Add Color

PAINTING

- Charcoal gray (Ceramcoat)
- Titanium white (Americana)
- Christmas red (Americana)
- Santa flesh (Ceramcoat)
- Earth brown (Anita's)
- French blue (FolkArt)
- Ebony black (Americana)
- Dolphin gray (Americana)
- Antique gold metallic (Accent Crown Jewels)
- Burnt sienna (Americana) and Santa flesh mixture

FINISHING

- Deft Clear Wood Finish Satin
- Watco Wax—mixture of neutral and dark

Front

Back

Left side

Right side

CARVING THE HAND

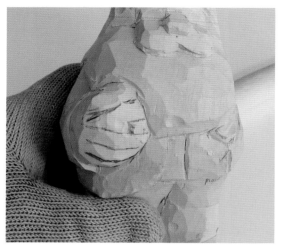

1. Rough out the right hand large enough so he can hold the candy stick. Draw in, with a pencil, the fingers and thumb.

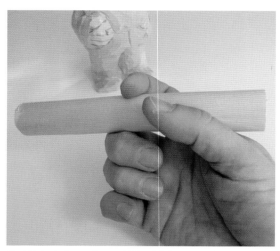

2. This is how he will hold his candy stick.

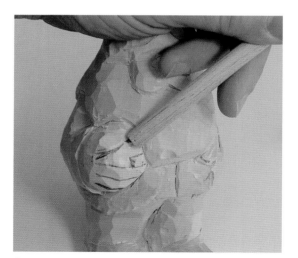

3. In this demonstration I use a ⅜ inch (9 mm) dowel as a demonstration. You can use a smaller dowel, preferably ¼ inch (6 mm).

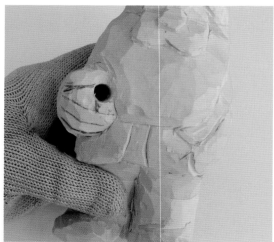

4. Drill a hole between the forefinger and thumb the diameter of your dowel.

5. Cut the dowel to desired length. Insert to verify the hole will fit the dowel.

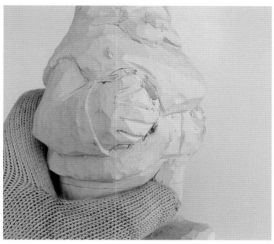

6. Use a V tool to chisel out the pencil marks. This is a good start in cutting out the fingers.

7. Cut the forefinger away from the middle finger and thumb.

8. Separate the top of the forefinger from the rest of the hand.

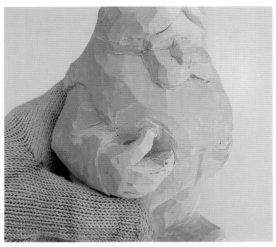

9. Separate the bottom of the pinky finger from the hand.

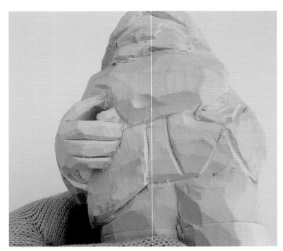

10. With the use of a knife, curl the fingers in.

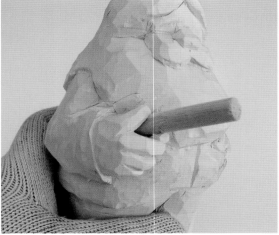

11. Use a knife to shape the fingers. Adjust so it looks like a hand holding a candy stick or cigar.

TOY STORE MANAGER SANTA PATTERN

Front   **Left Side**

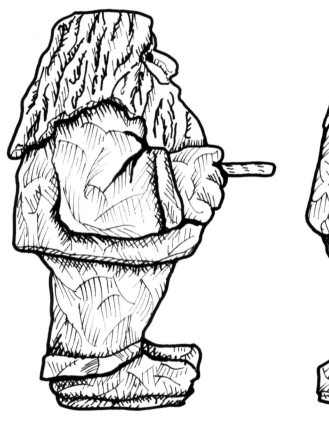

Right Side

Back

COLA SANTA (BONUS) PATTERN

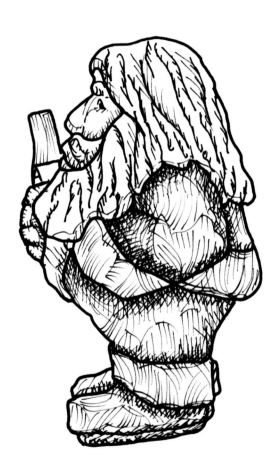

Front

Left Side

Right Side

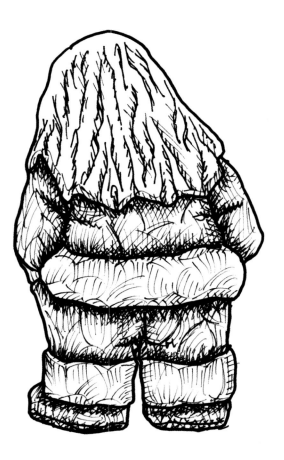

Back

Snowboard Santa

There's something about being outside in the cold, crisp air up on the slopes that makes me forget all about my responsibilities back at the North Pole. It's fast, invigorating, and maybe a little bit dangerous. Plus I love the scenery of snow-covered hills sparkling under a clear, blue sky, the majestic pine trees off to the sides, and the lifts carrying people all decked out in colorful winter gear to the top of the slope.

Add Color

PAINTING

- ⬤ Titanium white (Americana)
- ⬤ Holly green (Americana)
- ⬤ Ebony black (Americana)
- ⬤ Christmas red (Americana)
- ⬤ Santa flesh (Ceramcoat)
- ⬤ French blue (FolkArt)
- ⬤ Dolphin gray (Americana)
- ⬤ Burnt sienna (Americana) and Santa flesh mixture

FINISHING

- Deft Clear Wood Finish Satin
- Watco Wax—mixture of neutral and dark

Front

Back

Left side

Right side

ROUGH OUT THE FIGURE

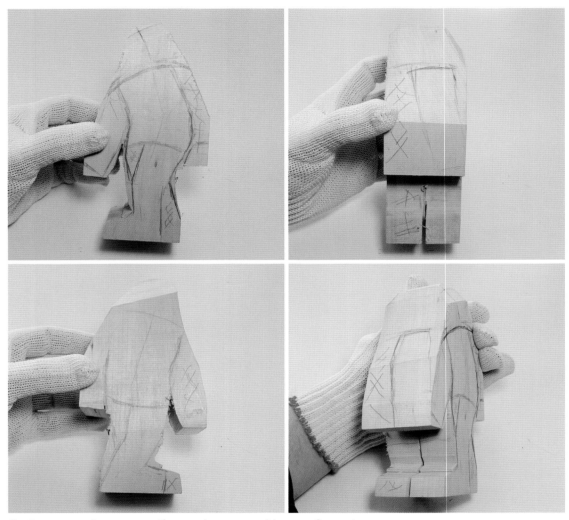

1. Cut out and use a pencil to make arm and leg configurations.

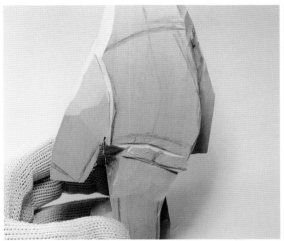

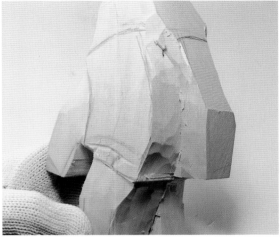

2. Block out hands and arms on all sides as shown.

3. Draw in the foot boot shape.

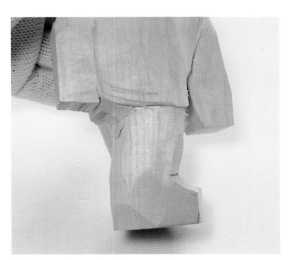

4. Round out the legs and boots.

BEGIN CARVING DETAILS

5. Round out the coat. Remember that the top half will twist around with the feet pointing in another direction.

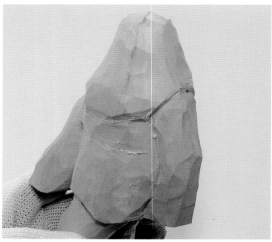

6. Round the head. Draw in the hair and the length of the beard, then V cut and carve up to the bottom of the beard.

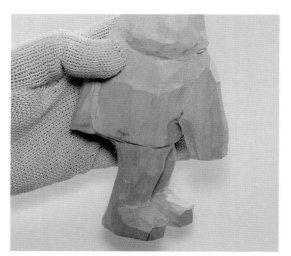

7. Draw in the boots and bottoms of the pants. Next, V cut and shape the shoes.

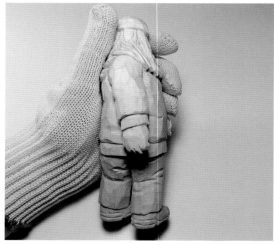

8. Carve in the details, especially the arm width and sleeves and creases.

SNOW AND SNOWBOARD TEMPLATES

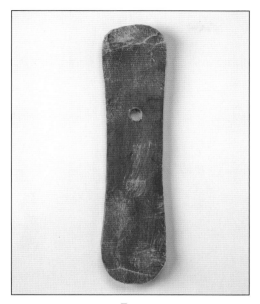

Top

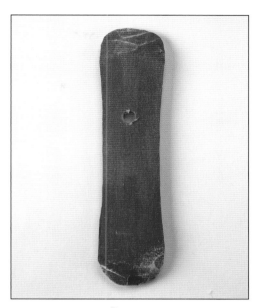

Bottom

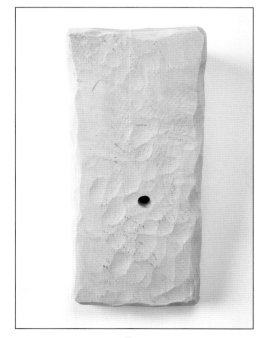

Top

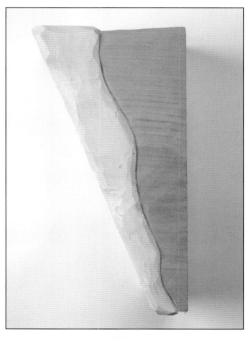

Side

SNOWBOARD SANTA PATTERN

Front

Left Side

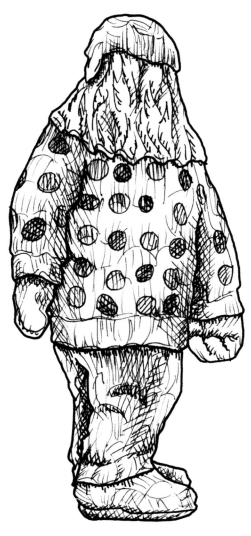

Right Side

Back

Librarian Santa

I love to spend time with the children who come to the library, by reading aloud to them or by helping them discover new books or authors. It brings me joy whenever a child returns to the library and (quietly) thanks me for a book suggestion I've made, and asks for further recommendations— fostering learning and imagination is my favorite part of my job.

Add Color

PAINTING

 Light avocado green (Americana)

Earth Brown (Anita's)

 Christmas red (Americana)

 Santa flesh (Ceramcoat)

 Titanium white (Americana)

French blue (FolkArt)

Ebony black (Americana)

Dolphin gray (Americana)

Burnt sienna (Americana) and Santa flesh mixture

FINISHING
- Deft Clear Wood Finish Satin
- Watco Wax—mixture of neutral and dark

Front

Back

Left side

Right side

ROUGH OUT THE FIGURE

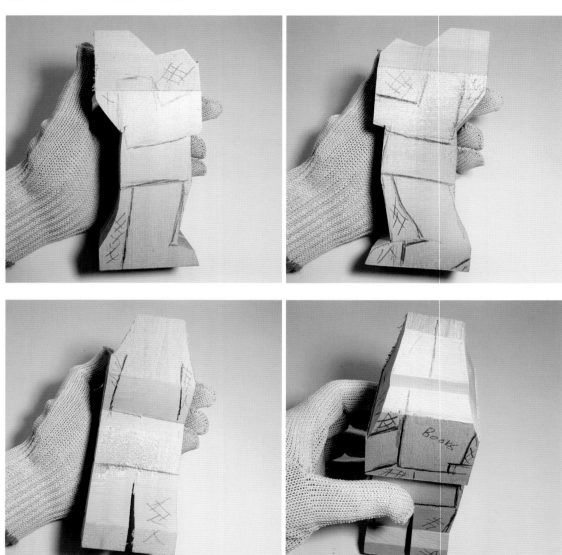

1. Cut out the rough shape of the figure then use a pencil to block out the sides and shoes.

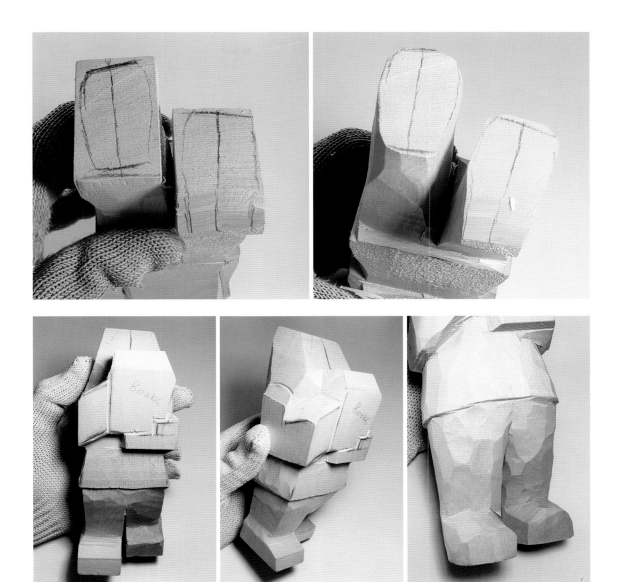

2. With your knife, round out the pants and shoes.

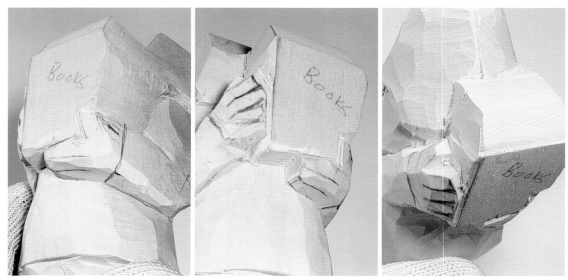

3. Pencil in the fingers.

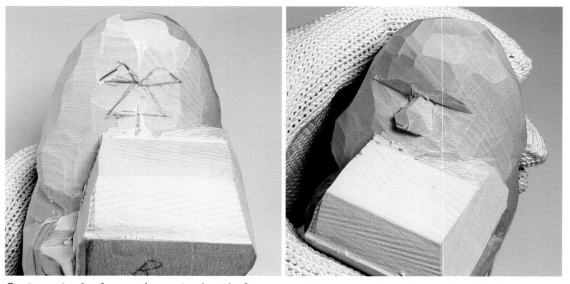

4. Carve in the face as shown in the Chef Santa carving instructions (pages 12–35). Keep in mind that the grain on this Santa's face may be a bit tricky.

CARVE THE BOOKS

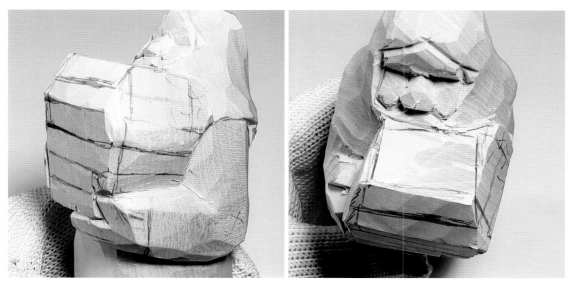

5. Use a pencil and mark straight lines to represent the books that the librarian is carrying.

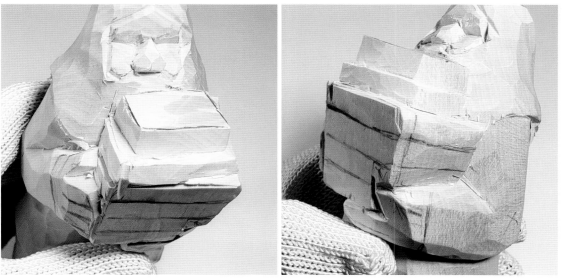

6. Start with the top book, V tool out the pencil marks, then use a knife to shape each book.

ADD DETAIL

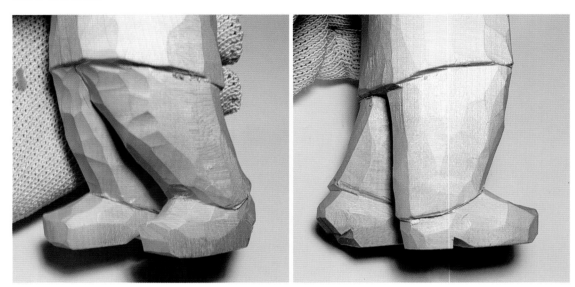

7. Shape the shoes. Remember, the left shoe's sole is lifted.

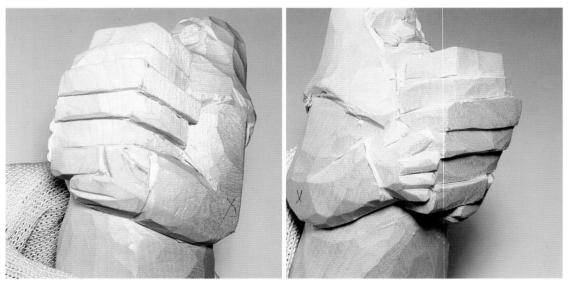

8. Use your V tool to chisel out the pencil marks showing the fingers, separating the fingers as shown.

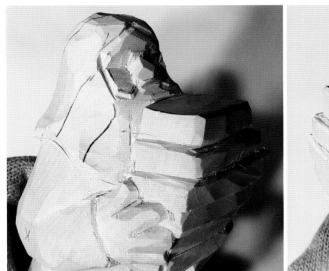

9. Mark out and carve his hair.

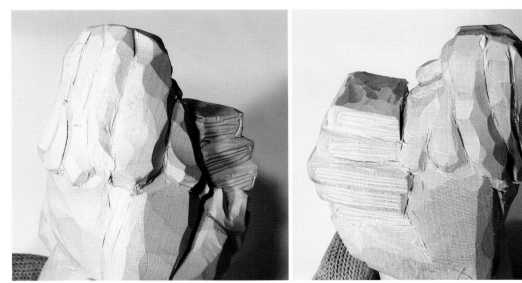

10. Mark straight lines to represent the books' covers and pages then carve. Continue shaping the hair.

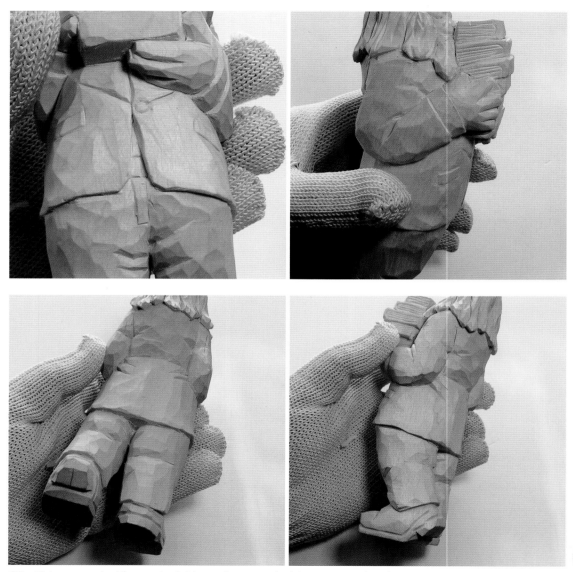

11. Using your knife, cut in folds and creases in his pants and jacket.

LIBRARIAN SANTA PATTERN

Front

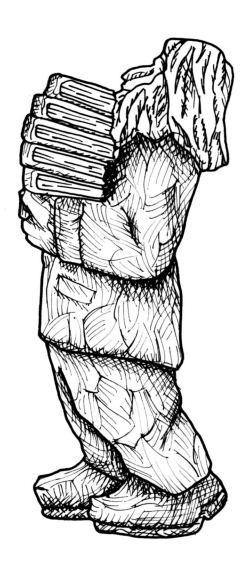

Left Side

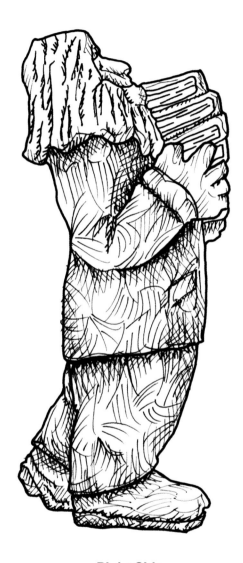

Right Side

Back

Fireman Santa

Matches and lighters are not toys, I always say during my fire safety presentations to children, and I remind people of the importance of staying back from heat sources such as stoves, furnaces, or campfires. I also go over checking smoke alarms to make sure they are working, the importance of having a home fire escape plan, the Stop, Drop, and Roll technique, and more. I'm used to getting a lot of questions!

Add Color

PAINTING

Yellow ochre (Americana)

Ebony black (Americana)

Christmas red (Americana)

Clover green (FolkArt)

Santa flesh (Ceramcoat)

Titanium white (Americana)

French blue (FolkArt)

Dolphin gray (Americana)

Burnt sienna (Americana) and Santa flesh mixture

FINISHING

· Deft Clear Wood Finish Satin
· Watco Wax—mixture of neutral and dark

Front

Back

Left side

Right side

ROUGH OUT THE FIGURE

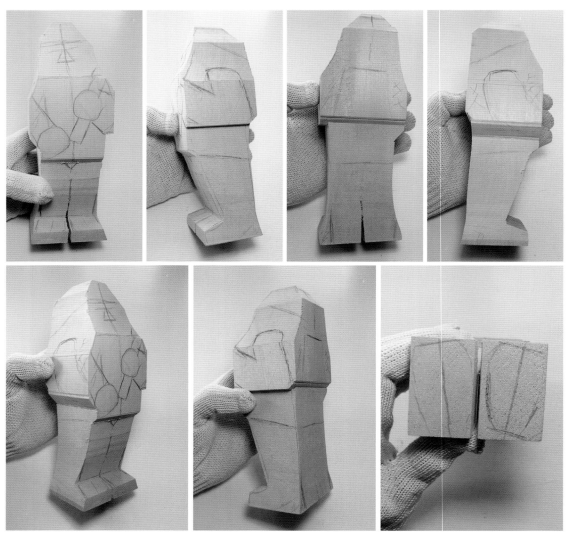

1. Cut out and use a pencil to make arm, leg, and shoe configurations.

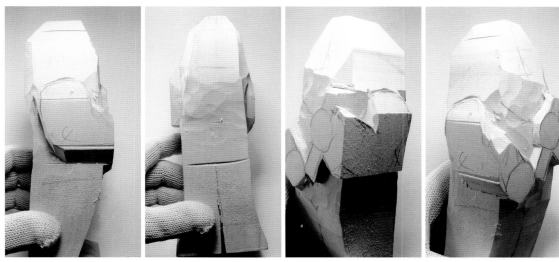

2. Block out the hands and arms on all sides, as shown.

3. Round out the coat, legs, and shoes.

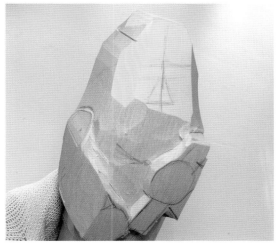

4. Round out the corners of the head. Carve up to the centerline of the face to make approximately a 45° angle.

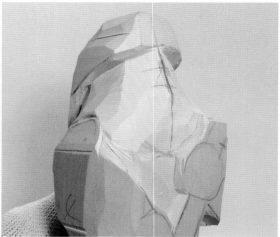

5. Draw then V cut the bottom rim of the hat; use a knife to make a stop cut then cut along the head up to the stop cut to bring the brim out.

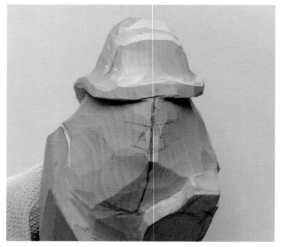

6. Draw then V cut the top rim of the hat, as shown.

7. Draw then V cut the front hat plate of the hat as shown, or to any desired shape.

CARVE THE FACIAL STRUCTURES

8. Use a pencil to draw triangles to represent the eye sockets and nose. Undercut the bottom of the nose down to his mustache.

9. Chip cut out the eye socket while bringing out the nose.

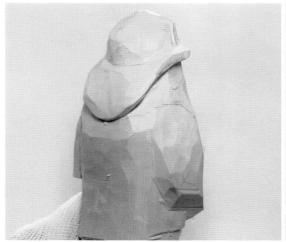

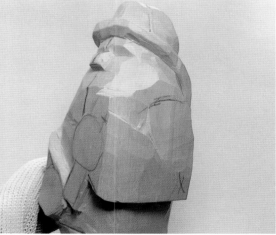

10. Carve inward—the upper arms to the shoulder—leaving the elbow protruding out.

CARVE THE HOSE

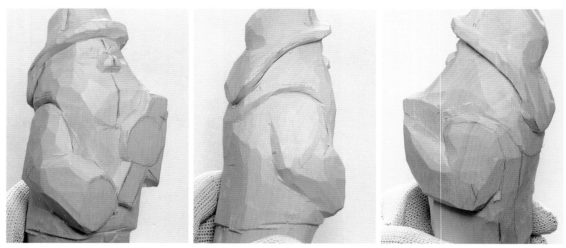

11. Round the arms. Draw in parallel lines from the hose spigot, over the shoulder, and down his back.

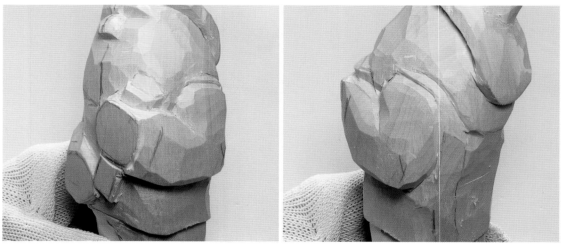

12. V cut the two parallel lines that will represent the hose.

13. Drill a hole through the right hand, which will hold the axe. Start with a small bit as a pilot hole and work your way up to a ¼ in. (6 mm) hole so you won't break the hand. Use a pencil to mark the four fingers on each hand so that they wrap around the hose nozzle and the axe.

 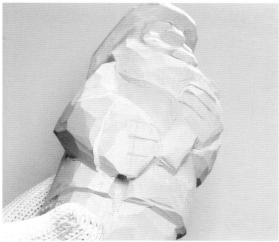

14. Press down on the side of the nose with a medium size #9 chisel to form the nostrils. Use the medium size #9 chisel to cut along the side of the nose from the tip to the eye socket. Use the medium size #9 chisel to cut along the top of the eye socket (under the eyebrow from the side, up in the middle of the stroke and down into the wood at the bridge of the nose, forming a bulge in the center. Use the same #9 chisel to shape the base of the nose and round the upper lid of the eye socket to the nose. Mark the side of the face and mustache. Use a V tool and cut out the pencil mark.

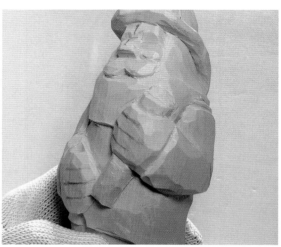

15. Firmly use your knife and cut down on the V lines to create a deep stop cut. Remove the wood under the mustache. Remove the wood from the sideburns to give the face depth. With the knife/chisel, round the eye socket on the outer sides of the face. (This is to remove the blockyness of the face for a more 3D effect.) Undercut the hat brim to make the hat look almost like a second piece of wood. You should see some shadow between the hat and hair.

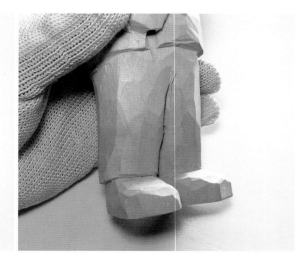

16. Use a knife to cut wood away from the shoe.

17. Draw a small semi-circle under the mustache for the mouth. Undercut the beard to the bottom of the mouth, bringing the bottom lip up. Use the tip of the knife to carve out the hole for the mouth (careful not to break the tip of the knife). Pencil in wavy lines on the beard and back hair. Make the lines come from the side of the face. Use a knife to make straight cuts drawn by the pencil. Use a knife and cut beard segments to a point. Use a knife to cut dents on both sides of the beard segments. Use a knife to undercut the tips of the beard segments to bring them out. Use a V tool and cut out definitions of the beard. Do not carve straight lines. Occasionally V cut crisscross lines to break up and parallel lines and make the beard scruffier. Use a V tool and cut out definitions of the mustache.

18. Draw in and V cut the pockets on both sides. Cut away some of the pants to bring out the pockets.

19. With a knife, cut in creases inside the legs. Pencil in and V cut rings around the pants legs. V cut the soles of the shoes.

20. V cut the pencil marks from the hands. Now you are finished!

MY PAINTING TIPS

There are many different methods for painting woodcarvings. Some people prefer a washed-out look that allows the wood to show through. They achieve that effect by using diluted paints. I prefer more intense colors so I mix less water with my acrylic paint. I also paint in layers to create more depth in my piece.

After completing a carving project I take the piece to a table with a lamp on either side, put on my best reading spectacles, and go over it with a sharp knife to remove any loose pieces, to clean up the corners, and to remove any pencil or saw marks. I then wash the piece using a small nail brush with dish soap and warm water to remove any oils from handling. The piece is then rinsed and allowed to dry.

Once dry I spray the piece with a light coat of matte finish. I prefer Deft brand, but I also use Rust-Oleum Painter's Touch. The finish keeps the paints from bleeding into each other and helps the paint spread evenly on the carving. Different areas of the wood may absorb the paint differently and the finish eliminates that problem. I allow the finish to dry before painting.

FIREMAN SANTA PATTERN

Front

Left Side

Right Side

Back

Basketball Coach Santa

At first, very few of my young players' shots end up anywhere near the net. Eventually, however, with practice, more of their shots are successful. Basketball gives children an opportunity to learn how to work together for the good of the team. Controlling emotions when opponents score, following the rules of the game, and keeping each other's spirits up are great lessons for kids to learn.

Add Color

PAINTING

French blue
(FolkArt)

Earth brown
(Anita's)

Navy blue
(FolkArt)

Ebony black
(Americana)

Titanium white
(Americana)

Dolphin gray
(Americana)

Cadmium
orange
(Americana)

Burnt sienna
(Americana)

FINISHING
· Deft Clear Wood Finish Satin
· Watco Wax—mixture of neutral and dark

Front

Back

Left side

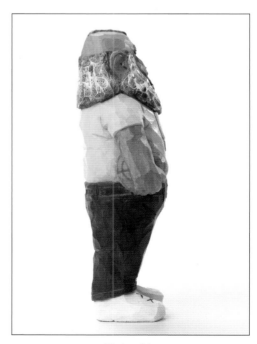

Right side

ROUGH OUT THE BEARD

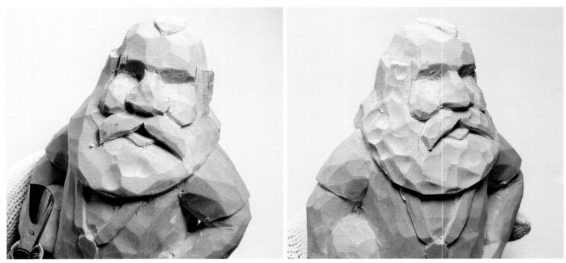

1. Shape the beard and hair in back to desired length and depth (or as shown). Use a medium size #9 chisel to make gouge cuts to roughen the beard.

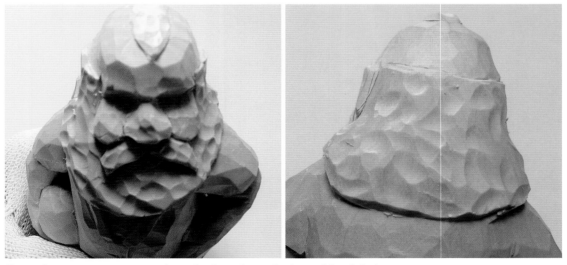

2. Make gouge cuts to roughen the beard, top hair, and back hair.

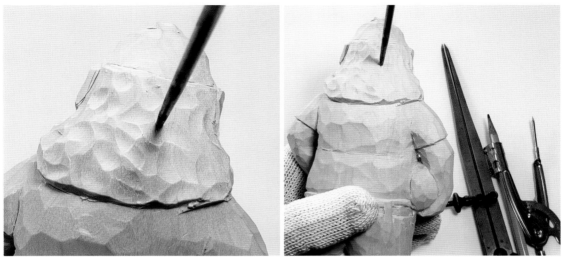

3. Make stipple holes with the use of a pointy tool such as an ice pick, divider, or compass.

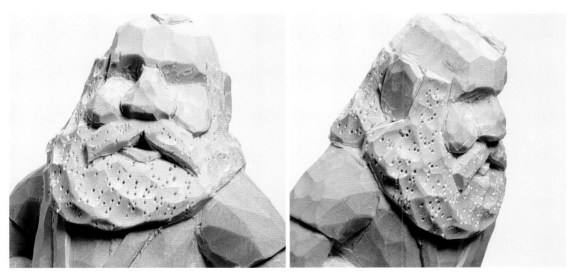

4. Make as many stipple holes as you can.

BASKETBALL COACH SANTA PATTERN

Front

Left Side

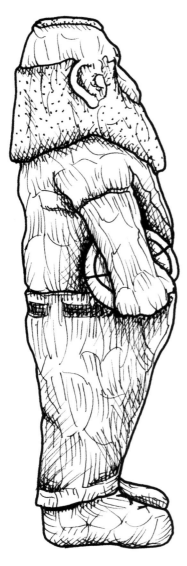

Right Side

Back

Mailman Santa

Walking the neighborhood as I deliver the mail, I have a full view of the schools, playgrounds, and even the back alleys. From these vantage points I see children in action and how they interact with each other. Most play nice, but the naughty kids have no idea I have my naughty-or-nice list handy in my mail pouch!

Add Color

PAINTING

 Navy blue (FolkArt)

 Antique gold (Accent Crown Jewel)

 Ebony black (Americana)

 Honey brown (Americana)

 Santa flesh (Ceramcoat)

 Titanium white (Americana)

French blue (FolkArt)

Dolphin gray (Americana)

 Burnt sienna (Americana) and Santa flesh mixture

FINISHING

- Deft Clear Wood Finish Satin
- Watco Wax—mixture of neutral and dark

Front

Back

Left side

Right side

MAILMAN SANTA PATTERN

Front

Left Side

Right Side

Back

School Nurse Mrs. Santa

Emotions run high or low when children have to come see me for exams or shots, and they need lots of patience and extra care from the adults at these times. I find it immensely rewarding when I can help ease pain or bring relief to a child who needs care.

Add Color

PAINTING

- French blue (FolkArt)
- Santa flesh (Ceramcoat)
- Titanium white (Americana)
- Ebony black (Americana)
- Primary blue (Americana)
- Dolphin gray (Americana)
- Christmas red (Americana)
- Burnt sienna (Americana) and Santa flesh mixture

FINISHING

- Deft Clear Wood Finish Satin
- Watco Wax—mixture of neutral and dark

Front

Back

Left side

Right side

SCHOOL NURSE MRS. SANTA PATTERN

Front

Left Side

Right Side

Back

Baseball Coach Santa

Childhood baseball games are a great American ritual. Finding or creating little improvised "baseball diamonds" around the neighborhood, getting teams together, and playing a structured game gives youngsters an outlet for their creativity. It's also a great way to learn cooperation and to get fresh air. My job is just to make sure everybody has fun.

Add Color

PAINTING

Primary blue (Americana)

French blue (FolkArt)

Titanium white (Americana)

Ebony black (Americana)

Christmas red (Americana)

Dolphin gray (Americana)

Nutmeg brown (Apple Barrel)

Burnt sienna (Americana) and Santa flesh mixture

Santa flesh (Ceramcoat)

FINISHING

- Deft Clear Wood Finish Satin
- Watco Wax—mixture of neutral and dark

Front

Back

Left side

Right side

BASEBALL COACH SANTA PATTERN

Front

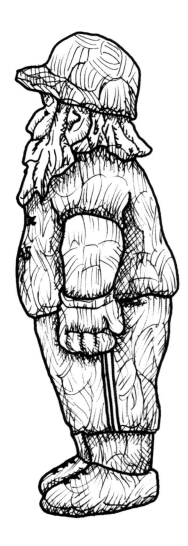

Left Side

Right Side

Back

Policeman Santa

I t's my responsibility to teach children the importance of practicing kindness to each another. Many times, the troublemakers are those who feel isolated and alone. Going out of your way to include other kids in your conversations or games goes a long way toward helping people feel a part of a group. The more included people feel, the easier my job is!

Add Color

PAINTING

- French blue (FolkArt)
- Titanium white (Americana)
- Primary blue (Americana)
- Ebony black (Americana)
- Christmas red (Americana)
- Dolphin gray (Americana)
- Earth brown (Anita's)
- Burnt sienna (Americana) and Santa flesh mixture
- Santa flesh (Ceramcoat)

FINISHING

- Deft Clear Wood Finish Satin
- Watco Wax—mixture of neutral and dark

Front

Back

Left side

Right side

POLICEMAN SANTA PATTERN

Front

Left Side

Right Side

Back

Tree Farmer Santa

Every year, on the day after Thanksgiving, I'm out at my Christmas tree farm, helping families with children pick out the trees that will be perfect for their homes. Around the bonfire, people gather to sip hot cocoa, coffee, or tea while munching on the sausages I made as they wait for wagon rides through the pine trees. It's chock full of Christmas spirit!

Add Color

PAINTING

- Christmas red (Americana)
- Titanium white (Americana)
- Primary blue (Americana)
- French blue (FolkArt)
- Christmas green (Americana)
- Ebony black (Americana)
- Metallic silver (FolkArt)
- Dolphin gray (Americana)
- Earth brown (Anita's)
- Burnt sienna (Americana) and Santa flesh mixture
- Santa flesh (Ceramcoat)

FINISHING

- Deft Clear Wood Finish Satin
- Watco Wax—mixture of neutral and dark

Front

Back

Left side

Right side

TREE FARMER SANTA PATTERN

Front

Left Side

Right Side

Back

Lifeguard Santa

At the beach or swimming pool, children are usually happy and excited. They have a large place to play and move around. Instead of sitting inside they can swim, jump into the water, play with water toys, and be noisy. My job is to keep my eyes open and watch out for people's safety at all times. It's also great to see so many people getting along so well.

Add Color

PAINTING

- Titanium white (Americana)
- French blue (FolkArt)
- Christmas red (Americana)
- Ebony black (Americana)
- Christmas green (Americana)
- Dolphin gray (Americana)
- Santa flesh (Ceramcoat)
- Burnt sienna (Americana) and Santa flesh mixture

FINISHING

- Deft Clear Wood Finish Satin
- Watco Wax—mixture of neutral and dar

Front

Back

Left side

Right side

LIFEGUARD SANTA PATTERN

Front

Left Side

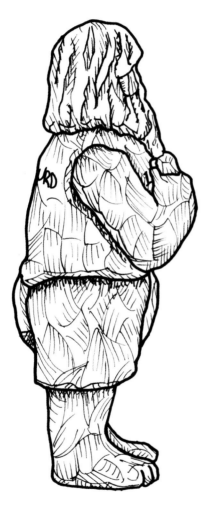

Right Side

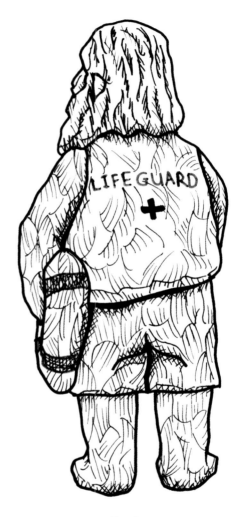

Back

About the Author

Russell Scott signed up for his first woodcarving class in 1999 through community education and loved it from the start. His first teacher assigned six carving projects in the eight-week class using hand tools only and a wide selection of woods (basswood, catalpa, red cedar, butternut, aspen and pine). The final class project was a Santa Claus figure. Russ thought his first Santa carving was a masterpiece.

Since that time he has taken many carvings classes from a wide range of instructors (locally and nationally), studied books, videos and carving magazines. He has carved and consulted with other woodcarvers through the years from whom he learned many techniques and methods for carving, painting and finishing. He has developed his own style of carving and specializes in carving human figures, especially Santa Claus.

Each carving is done entirely by hand, carved free form from a model that Russ has developed using computer software and drawings. He carves mostly in basswood and cottonwood bark. After carving each character, Russ uses paint to enhance the image. His carvings have received awards at carving shows, county and state fairs, and national carving contests. He is a member of several professional carving organizations. Russ also teaches woodcarving classes and has written several instructional woodcarving books and created videos which can be viewed on YouTube (see next page).

Helpful Resources

My Woodcarving Classes

I teach woodcarving through my videos on YouTube, my books, and through my classes using rough-outs of my original designs. If you're interested in jumping to the next level in your woodcarving artistry, then check out my class schedules, instructional books and videos and try your hand using one of my basswood rough-outs.

You can find me at:

- *www.ScottCarvings.com*
- *www.youtube.com/user/scottcarvings*

National Resources

- The National Wood Carvers Association (NWCA) publishes a newsletter called *Chip Chats, chipchats.org.*
- *Woodcarving Illustrated* (magazine by Fox Chapel Publishing): *woodcarvingillustrated.com*, source for information on products, classes, meetings, and carvers.
- Woodcarving Warehouse is run by Chris Whillock and based out of Faribault, Minnesota. *www. woodcarverswarehouse.com*.
- International Woodcarvers Congress, Maquoketa, Iowa, *www.awcltd.org*, featuring national instructors and students.
- Carv-Fest, Faribault, *carv-fest.com*, also featuring national instructors and students.

Index